ART AND OUTRAGE

HENRY MILLER

[Photo by Arthur Knight

ART
AND OUTRAGE

A correspondence about Henry Miller

between
ALFRED PERLÈS
and
LAWRENCE DURRELL

(With an intermission by Henry Miller)

PUTNAM
42 GREAT RUSSELL STREET
LONDON MCMLIX

Made and printed in Great Britain
by Richard Clay and Company, Ltd., Bungay, Suffolk
for the Publishers, Putnam and Company Ltd.

Contents

From Lawrence Durrell

to Alfred Perlès

My dear Joe,

I began this letter to you in my head some four years ago when chance took me through Paris for a few hours on my way to Yugoslavia. It was born precisely during an evening walk among a dozen prose water-colours of Paris by Henry Miller, recollected in the tranquillity of a dusk which borrowed its colours from one of those gem-like paragraphs in *Tropic of Cancer*. Do I need to tell you that I was in the precincts of Villa Seurat where we spent so many exciting months together? The little tin *vespasienne* with its ads for Quinquina still stands at the road-junction. Ditto the lamp-post under which, one foggy dusk, I saw the *cher maitre* standing spellbound by the pages of Nijinsky which I had just brought back from London, reading in the street. I think it was the night when you destroyed Madame Kalf's plumbing and the Chinese editor of the *Booster* ran screaming out into the night to disappear forever and deprive us of the article he had promised us on Some Confucian Confusions. . . . To walk in this milky dusk with the smoke rising from the *bistro*. Click of billiard balls, clink on the zinc of white wine glasses, chipping of billiard balls, and somewhere a ghostly radio playing a long-lost jazz tune, preserved in the affections of the French by some haphazard tenderness of the words. . . .

It is many years since then and I am in a different place now, the rain pattering down among the vines and the voice of Henry (recorded on discs) sounding as warm as ever on the dusk; the voice of an American Academician whose works are denied entry to his own country—could anything characterise Anglo-Saxondom better? There he sits, the lone American eagle in his eyrie at Big Sur, still writing for the French and the Japanese! One is forced to laugh, albeit a little sadly. What has poor Henry done that Columbus didn't? His journey has been a far more heroic one for at the end of it he has discovered himself—the unknown Americas of the American soul. But in order to do so he had been forced to outrage the sensibilities of his contemporaries, to force the steel locks of the tabu, to batter and thrash like a stricken whale, to twist and bend and hammer. . . . And now he has broken through, he is canonised! Recognised as the greatest example of American genius since Whitman. But . . . the books won't get through yet awhile!

I was thinking over the injustice of this situation which made me wonder whether we could not, between us, do something to put the totality of his work into perspective for the Anglo-Saxon reader. How would one gauge the value of Lawrence if only his travel books were allowed to circulate? All that is known of Henry *chez nous* is a series of anthologies of short stories and essays—dense and rich to be sure; but the two great trilogies are missing from the count. So it is that you may pick up a 5000-word survey of modern American literature without ever once happening upon his name. And American literature today begins and ends with the meaning of what he has done. I don't want to denigrate Faulkner, Hemingway, etc., but they are simply literary journeymen like ourselves. There is a qualitative difference between the obsessional power of genius and the head-contrivances of us folk. Not that I think the journeyman bad—on the contrary he makes the humus out of which the genius can flower. It takes a hundred of us to manufacture the subsoil in which a genius can grow.

Walking these shabby and beloved streets, I thought I would drop you a line and see whether I could tempt you into a correspondence which might result in a portrait— not of the man, for you have done that already—but of the artist, mirrored in his work. After all, you and I are in the position of lucky clerks who enjoyed the intimacy of Rabelais. His conversations! What would the world not give for some more details than the few which are available to-day?

My idea is somewhat reinforced by reading your portrait of

Henry because in it you side-step the purely critical questions, the evaluations, in order the better to concentrate on the likeness of the man. You admit that there is an element of mystery and leave it at that, and who can say you are wrong? Certainly the central mystery of a creative personality cannot be circumscribed completely. But in thinking of the whole span and wealth of his work from *Tropic of Cancer* to the latest Japanese water-colour on sex could we, informally and without preciousness, get any closer? I suppose temperamental differences account for each one's angle of vision on a given person. Reading that anthology, *The Happy Rock*, I was very much struck by the number of different Henry-faces which emerged; they were all Henry to be sure—but refracted by the observer. Am I too guilty of wilful refraction in stressing how unlike himself is the Henry of the books? It comes as a shock to people questioning me when I draw the portrait of a man so gentle, loyal and tender; and a man with such a finely spun sensibility that if ever he put a foot wrong it was from sheer nerves. The lovable childlike qualities which included an ability to be cast-down by the slightest rebuff! Then the positive side—the aggressions and savageries which always get thrown up under the stress of creative work, the twisted complex of childhood distortions and fears; the bitterness which was always melted into the happiest laughter I have ever heard?

No, it was not an exchange of anecdotes which I intended, either. Though here and there they too might help—like your story of his first public lecture! But I wondered vaguely whether one might trace the outlines of another sort of picture —that which came to my mind walking about these streets. *Is art always an outrage*—must it by its very nature be an outrage?

It was time to catch my train, but I lingered reluctantly under the church at Alésia, reflecting on the nature of Henry's particular struggle with ink and paper. Its very violence contains a lesson which the wise reader will be able to interpret to himself. 'Truth' I want to get to, the Truth about myself!

How much or how little truth did he find on the way—on

this long journey from the position of an American Villon to that of Chuang Tzu?

I wonder if these lines will tempt you to your typewriter up there in windy Hampstead?

Larry.

From Alfred Perlès

to Lawrence Durrell

Dear Larry,

I'm all for it—naturally. The idea is fascinating and, moreover, there's a sporting chance of such a correspondence as you suggest yielding at least an approximate portrait of the artist. As a matter of fact, if Henry the artist, or rather the genius, can be caught at all in his processive phases, there are probably no other two men in the world better equipped to do the catch than you and I. *Et pour cause:* for amongst his thousand and one friends who walk in and out of his books and letters as in a milk bar, we are no doubt the two most articulate ones to have witnessed the unfolding of his genius from puberty to maturity; and he has given us enough hints to trace it back to childhood and the ever-present Devachan.

But how are we to proceed? Your mentioning of streets and tin *vespasiennes* is not a bad opening gambit. A wine list might conveniently be added and the names of the *cinémas du quartier*, perhaps also Madame Kalf's telephone number and the smell and flavour of garlic in the delicious *escargot* restaurant off the rue d'Alésia. And then, what? Do we begin at the beginning or in the Villa Seurat? I think it is important that we synchronise our memories for the venture we're embarking on. Your entry on the scene dates from Villa Seurat, mine goes back to 1bis rue du Maine, some ten years earlier. It's all the same party of course, but you know how it is when one gets stone sober to a party that is already in full swing. What I mean is that, metaphorically speaking (and perhaps not so metaphorically, either), I was already in a state of advanced inebriety when you joined us. But perhaps you weren't so stone sober yourself? There are emanations that go a long way, and with protracted delayed-action effect.

All the same, let me pinpoint the period. Villa Seurat, in my memory, was already superimposed by a pretty pattern of street names and hotels of the 5th, 6th, 13th, and 16th *arrondissements*, as well as Dijon, Clichy, Louveciennes and Marnes-la-Coquette, when you showed up. At the time of your sensational entry in the Villa Seurat the cat was practically in the bag. Things were already running smoothly, the cocoon was cut, the butterfly out of its chrysalis. What qualifies and at the same time impedes me in this correspondence, are the antecedents, the incubating period that led up to Villa Seurat with its tin *pissotières*, its sawdust restaurants and horoscope charts. At the centre of my memory there's the Hotel Central where I read the opening pages of number one version of *Cancer* as they came out of the typewriter in the room next door to mine. Can you imagine the terrific impact they made on a semi-literate Balkanese like myself? It was then that I had my first inkling of the presence of genius in the man: a revelation as miraculous as the apparition of the lady in the grotto. I had a sudden glimpse of his reality. And this reality is still real, incredibly, imperishably real!

That's where the impediment comes in: I owe him too much! How can one do justice to a man to whom one owes too much? He took me in his school and made a pupil of me. No Michelangelo apprentice could have felt prouder, happier. He gave me the facts of life, a language, a mode of expression, and a trauma or two, for good measure. All the shocks I owe him have turned traumatic and when I listen to his speech, as I now do via the L.P. record player, the timbre of his voice works on me like a hypnotic reminder that I have graduated into discipleship.

Well, the disciple has a duty to fulfil, if only to write a gospel. I've done it once but as you know it didn't quite come off. I've portrayed the man and scamped his work, hoping the man would mirror his work. Of course, it doesn't—not even in the case of Henry whose work and personality are almost (but not totally) intertwined. And that's why I feel so grateful to you for offering me the opportunity of completing the job in these letters. I have in the past been rather averse to criticism, subconsciously confusing criticism with blame. But I now realize that Henry can only be recognized for the genius he is if we disentangle him, critically, from the stupid pornographic legend and present him to the Anglo-Saxon reader in his essential innocence. For genius is essentially innocent, even—and perhaps especially—when it is outrageous: as innocent as an earthquake or an erupting volcano. In our present task the value of genuine literary criticism lies precisely in pointing this out.

But you'll have to take the lead, Larry. I'm convinced that you could write this correspondence all by yourself, perhaps even better than with my partnership, but if you think I can add to the picture I'll try and do my best. The least I can do is to react like a highly sensitized photographic plate to the quartz rays of your mind: I can conceive provided I'm fertilised.

Fred.

P.S. At the mention of innocence, an idea strikes me: would you say it is Henry's innocence that makes for his so often uneven writing? Writers of lesser magnitude, the literary journeymen as you call them, are *not* uneven: they are far too much concerned with style to produce unpolished gems. But between Balzac and Dostoevski and before and after (always excluding Goethe who was a Virgo type) a lot of shockingly bad writing has been committed by geniuses, though without detriment to the ensemble effect. The innocence of the eruption again: the volcano spews out gems and ashes indiscriminately, it's a matter of take it or leave it, no?

Fr.

From Lawrence Durrell

to Alfred Perlès

Dear Joe,

Yes, of course I realise the handicaps as well as the advantages of your knowledge, and I think you have acquitted yourself very honourably in the book—which I have been rifling again. Particularly the physical descriptions, which are first rate. Nor did I have in mind any rambling exchange of letters on general ideas. Rather a few 'establishing shots' as they say in movies of this interesting subject. I am thinking really of the long arguments in words and on paper which I have endured with his readers, and particularly his young readers. Out of them all two things emerge clearly. In the first place the *intentions* of his work and its meaning often don't get through: I mean his books are simply regarded as a brilliant display of temperament, of gift. Secondly I always find myself defending him against the portrait he has given of himself! This really is rather queer! 'But he's not like that at all!' I catch myself saying. What, then, is he like? Certainly I recognise him from his own description—but I see much else beside. And the amusing thing is that Henry himself gets plaintive at times when he is called 'a Genghis Khan' or a 'cannibal'! This of course makes me laugh and swear, because if once you knock down all the windmills of morality how can you thereafter not expect the moralist to hold his nose? And now in these discs comes the most perfect thing—'As a matter of fact I have deliberately left out of my work all the better, all the bigger side of myself, from what you might call a sense of *pudeur*'! This is, or should be, the *boutade* of the century—if it has sprung from the lips of an ironist. Henry Miller, the pudic writer! But what makes me laugh and swear is that this is a plain statement of fact. What do you say?

That is why at the back of my mind I was wondering whether

14

we could not do him the service of situating the scheme of his work within the scope of an intention, and at the same time try and give an account of the bewildering collection of masks from which he speaks? Some of it you have done; but I think if I could rustle up your memory a bit you would find other treasures which might help to reveal him a little more clearly. If we could do this in a booklet or pamphlet without too much critical jargon it might be of service to the younger reader today. But I do agree about the handicaps which come from realising the sheer size of one's subject. With genius the *pour* and *contre* count for very little indeed; and art reserves its greatest treasures for those who forget its existence. I myself always felt rather like Palmer who says that he could never call upon Mr. Blake without first kissing the knob on the door before knocking! There was unfortunately no door-knob on the Villa Seurat studio, and the inhabitant of that memorable room did not stand in need of disciples but friends. A hundred years from now we won't be forgiven for not putting down as best we can the little we know of him and the line of wild country which he undertook to explore single handed—don't you think?

This, then, is very roughly what I had in mind. Nor do I think there is need for haste. Let the letters ebb and flow as they will, and let us scribble into the picture anything we think as relevant to the portrait—what do you say? And let us print our disagreement, if any, as they come. . . . A carbon to the unfortunate subject also, in case he would like to intervene and bang our heads together!

First, then, the work which stretches across the barren landscape of contemporary literature in some great weird parabola. Would his intentions be better illustrated by a glance at other solipsists who have chosen an autobiographical form of self-expression? Casanova had a good deal more *volupté*, Rousseau, De Sade . . . would this be a fruitful starting point? Am I wrong in picking out one major difference in Henry—a religious intention, perhaps even unknown to himself? I wonder to what extent he was influenced by (or agreed with) Otto Rank's ideas in ART AND ARTIST. I still have a copy which he and Anaïs gave me for my birthday with an inscription. Now for Rank art was going into a new phase which was characterised by what he calls 'personality-development' which would not be expressed in outward forms but by inward growth . . . I am only groping here because the path that the books cut runs directly from the fleshly to the spiritual nature; there is a solution, so to speak, as there never is in the morality-obsessed De Sade. Both he and Henry dismantled the morality of their ages; but Henry's intention was to question it and reformulate his own. He progresses, grows, exfoliates as a personality. De Sade stays put like an electronic device which has got stuck. The cry of anguish behind his work is always: 'Look, there is no morality in nature. I can prove it to you.' Satiety, boredom and disgust are the bedfellows of the tiresome Marquis. How an educated Japanese would laugh over him. But Henry gets somewhere through the tremendous tangle and jumble of his work with its extraordinary heights and depths. Is it the laughter that helps him grow? His resemblance to Rabelais? Nor can I deny that he doesn't sometimes set my own teeth on edge in exactly the way Panurge does!

It seems to me that somewhere the basic intention is a spiritual search in the course of which he dismantles and shreds up the physical body in order to transcend it. Am I wrong in suspecting him of being, so to speak, an inverted moralist—or rather a man in search of a scheme of values which might represent something like a morality of the soul? At any rate he has escaped from the tiresome rat-trap of the Marquis and achieved —or says he has—a kind of *rapport* with the rhythms of nature— an issue where the creative man and the literary follow the same road.

Is this the light in which he should be read? Ouf! I am not trying to make a literary thesis out of him. I remember him writing to me once 'My work represents germination in *all* its phases'!

Would I be further from the mark if I suspected in him the strong puritan back-lash which all we Anglo-Saxons have? He has dealt the central motives of our cultural puritanism a

mortal blow in his books, and in freeing us has also freed himself. Like Lawrence he exclaimed: 'O why do the English fence
off the great wild scope of their natures?'!

Discuss please, using one side of the paper only!

Larry.

B

From Alfred Perlès

to Lawrence Durrell

Dear Larry,

You ask me, and yourself, what he's like, but I'm afraid there's no ready answer. And if he himself told you what he was like his answer could not but be misleading. What's a kaleidoscope like if not unto itself? Always different but always the kaleidoscope: a million and one facets upon which, turn by turn, an accenting ray puts a varying emphasis. The attempt to coagulate all the possible image combinations into one rigid picture is as hopeless as trying to gauge the number and scope of all the books that can be written with the 26 letters of the alphabet. The number is infinite, and we'd be wasting our time looking for Henry in a haystack of Henrys. The *Happy Rock*, as you observed in your previous letter, reflects only an infinitesimal fraction of Henrys, all valid, none complete.

To get at his essence, a different approach seems necessary. Just interpreting the *intentions* of his work, does not strike me as efficacious for the purpose, either. For what exactly *are* his intentions? Has he any, in the first place? I'm inclined to doubt it. Intention diminishes the artist. Genius is unintentional. The sun does not *intend* to radiate heat, it radiates it. To my perhaps illogical thinking the term 'intention' savours of propaganda, proselytism, promotion of ideas, etc., and somehow I prefer to think of Henry's work as intentionless. It's this intentionlessness, too, which accounts for his multiple 'masks'!

As for his autobiographical form of self-expression, can you conceive a work of art—a poem, a symphony, or even a novel—that is not autobiographical? Any true work of art must needs be of an autobiographical nature, except perhaps in the case of a cathedral, which is anonymous. But none of Henry's masks can be said to be anonymous. *Alors?* His solipsism cannot be compared, by way of situating him in the mountain range of literature, with that of other autobiographers, if for no other reason than his uniqueness. Apart from their respective uniqueness I can see no affinity between Henry, Rousseau, De Sade, Casanova etc. His sense of humour is only superficially germane to Rabelais's; for apart from the four centuries between them there's also a difference in the emphasis of their sense of humour: Henry's humour was born in the guts, Rabelais's in Holy Orders. And I refuse to consider Henry's evolution from the fleshly to the spiritual as a significant trait. Normally, such evolution would strike me as slightly suspect; nothing easier than to turn 'spiritual' a fortnight before impotence sets in. Of course, this isn't Henry's case: the spiritual is always latent in the flesh and vice versa, even in the rowdiest passages of the *Tropics*. If a genius can at all be akin to any other genius, which I doubt, I should compare him to Till Eulenspiegel or the Hauptmann Von Köpernick rather than any of the solipsists you mention. In the exploits of the legendary captain, especially, there is something of the *acte-gratuit* nonchalance which, transposed to the literary level, is strongly reminiscent of Henry's narrative writings.

Why is it, I keep asking myself, that I am so wary of tackling him from a purely literary point of view? It isn't that I have nothing to say about him as a writer—far from it! But is it, should it be, our object to restrict these epistolary exchanges to literary criticism? There will always be critics, even a hundred years hence, ready and eager to dissect, analyse, interpret and misinterpret his work, but there won't always be you and I who knew the man before he turned into a legend. If we want to do him a service I feel we must look at his work through the man and pin him down without any possible literary loopholes. Unless we succeed in doing that the clue to his work would still be missing.

Let me put it another way; Henry's work, in its ensemble, strikes me as a huge crossword puzzle which can only be solved correctly if solved differently by each of his serious readers. Our job is to give them the clues, the 6 across, and 3 down etc. But they must fill in the words themselves; I dare say they prefer it this way. I, for one, get always irritated when some busybody leaning over my shoulders prompts me when I do the *Times* crosswords. Each of the clues we thus give would point to one of the 'masks'. No fear that we will unmask him completely but if we can manage to tear off, say fifty or seventy masks out of five or nine hundred, *ça sera toujours ça de gagné, non*?

To come to the point, I feel that Henry Miller is one of those peculiar geniuses who must be approached from the human rather than the literary end; it is the human being, in all his aspects, who reveals the artist, explains the genius. The failure of literary criticism, at least in England and America, to gauge the portent of his work, to apprehend the fundamental simplicity of his writings, is due to the fact that Henry cannot be shanghaied into any literary category. The critics, sensing that they're up against some intangible force, resent this and half unconsciously try to diminish his worth, attacking now his *simpliste* attitude, now his bogus philosophy, now his pornography. I am not trying to belittle the critics, who have no doubt been to the best schools and are certainly no morons. But it is easy for them to scoff at him: it's easy to scoff at a quack in all civilised sincerity and indignation, even when the quack achieves results in hopeless cases where the bona fide doctors give up in despair. Don't forget that it takes a hundred years, and often longer, for a saint to get canonised.

It is a fact that Henry invariably appeals to the pure at heart—to simple human beings albeit ignoramuses. That letter you sent me from Alexandros Venetikos, guardian of the Phaestos ruins, is significant in this respect: as significant as the hundreds of letters he received as personnel manager of the Western Union long before his first book was published (I believe we reprinted one of those letters in the *Booster*); as significant, too, as your urge to kiss the non-existing door knob at Villa Seurat. It is the love he inspires in the hearts of simple human beings which stands at the threshold of his genius. It is this love, too, which accounts for the fact that his genius does not always get through in his works. It is useless, therefore, to argue about him with those young men you mention, whose traditional and cultural pragmatism removes them from Henry's intrinsic vision. But the Alexandros Venetikoses will always sense his genius in their hearts and succumb to his colossal impact where the critics turn up their noses at him in refined disgust.

The clues. . . . Has it ever struck you how serious he always is in his commerce with children? I am not thinking now of his own children (though I had occasion to observe him in his intercourse with Tony and Val, which I found rather revelatory of the man); I am thinking of the trust he used to put in children long before he had any of his own. Walking the Paris streets with him I was often surprised when he would go to a child for directions rather than a grown-up or an *agent de police*, who might have directed him much better. Sometimes he would address a very small street urchin who couldn't possibly, one might think, have known what he wanted and was at first inclined to start screaming at his atrocious accent. Yet he always elicited an intelligent answer in the end; not even the most infantile practical joker would have sent him on a wild-goose chase for the street round the corner. I couldn't help marvelling at this. There was something about him, something of the endearing alienness of the spaceman, that conquered the malice of the most moronic infant. He brought the goodness out of the child, if you know what I mean: the same goodness he later brought out of Mademoiselle Claude (who was a whore), and Max (who was a spiv). And this, it seems to me, is a significant clue to Henry the human being *and* the artist. Why is it that he was always surrounded by morons and helpless neurotics if not to make them whole again, at least in his writings? Those he couldn't make whole, the Borises etc., had only themselves to blame: you can't cure a leper if the leper refuses to believe he's suffering from leprosy.

You seem amazed at Henry's self-confessed *pudeur* but the thing doesn't come as a surprise to me; I always knew it was there. I should imagine that every real artist has it. In the lesser artist it assumes the guise of tact or nicety. It isn't modesty, for no modest person could talk about his *pudeur* in the context Henry does. *Pudeur*, in the sense he probably means it, is not a sense of shame, an obscure remnant of the original sin, but a sort of priestly reluctance to reveal the contents of the tabernacle. For Henry, who doesn't adhere to any religious sect, who has torn up his spiritual passport as it were, is high-priest nevertheless. God, with him, suffers no intermediary; his footprints are all over Mount Sinai.

Fred.

From Lawrence Durrell

to Alfred Perlès

Dear Joe,

      I agree with you about 'intentions' in the sense of conscious and didactic purpose of a moral or philosophic kind. I meant something like *gestalt*—for of course our author is himself growing with his work, and his views about its own scope and meaning have broadened and deepened since the day when, with *Tropic Of Cancer*, he cracked through the sound-barrier and found himself; he himself described *Tropic* as a gob of spit, a kick in the pants to Art, Truth etc. And there is no denying that it is a destructive book in a fecundating sense; but if it is tonic and inspiring it is because of the exultation that shines through it—the exultation of someone who revaluated the basic human values for himself, and emerged with a human morality of his very own, founded in his own bodily and spiritual experience.

I would not press any such general criticism on you (you know I hate criticism) were it not for the fact that we are discussing works which are not available to the reader, and it seems to me rather important to establish that Henry isn't another Sade or another Restif. Wherein does he differ? I think it important to stress that he is primarily a religious writer —which sounds of course a laughable paradox. And here I come to what I would call the basic intention behind his use of obscenity. He has effected an imaginative junction between the obscene and the holy—not exactly a new thing to the East but new and rather off-putting to the prurient West. The Ancient Greeks, for example ... There was a shrine to Heracles in Rhodes which the devout could only approach uttering a whole litany of obscenities! In Rozanov I read that the central mystery of the Jewish faith centres about a word (did he call it 'mikvah'? I have no books here) which is both the holiest and the most obscene of words at the same time. It is some of this terror and mystery that Henry conveys I think in his self-confessions and I suspect that later ages may read *Sexus*, parts of which are quite horripilating, with some of the patient awe that devotees visit those great Indian rock-cathedrals with their obscene-religious sculpture. Don't you think this is worth saying? At least someone who grasps the point will come to his work alertly and without prejudice and not feel he is just being insulted and spat upon. . . . I also think this factor explains Henry's own passion for the Eastern religious systems, for only these holy men would be able to read his spiritual adventure without prejudice, and would regard his books as a spiritual autobiography. A Japanese public seems no accident to me.

This is, to me, doubly important to state as in books like *Sexus* there is no specific statement of any such intention, and one has to read his essays out of the corner of the eye in order to sense the truth. Myself I had reservations about *Sexus* which turned upon this point; I felt that he had taken all the data about himself as equally important simply because it happened to him, and that a good deal of it added nothing to the pattern of this important book; it lay there unevaluated, as it were. But this is a criticism of craft. But the key to everything seems to me to be self-liberation and self-discovery—an important religious and artistic bias of mind. And surely this is what Keyserling meant by the telegram he sent him. ('I salute a free spirit').

Nor could he have been anything but an Anglo-Saxon writer for only here and there in Europe does the printer's tabu have the same power as over ourselves and the Americans; the French, for example, are never shocked—but either interested or just plain disgusted. I think in *Sexus* a Frenchman would only deplore lack of volupté and tenderness. He doesn't look out for the 'morally ennobling' but is rapidly disgusted by the coarseness of the Anglo-Saxon psyche. Moreover he sees most of our strains and stresses as fundamentally *laughable*—the result of living the wrong way. I have always found that the struggle of Lawrence isn't easily comprehended in Europe, because the Europeans are adults and are more amused than frightened of people in their pipi caca stage. But whether the French critics have evaluated Henry in these terms (I mean the religious) I don't really know; or whether they admire him as a tremendous creative writer. They are rather prone to admire a talent at the expense of a new temperament, a creative man *sui generis*.

This said, only a line or two about the masks. Certainly I did see several people peeping out of Henry. The most endearing were of course the childish ones—the clown, the American tourist, the gullible one (deliberately: did ever anyone enjoy so much being 'taken in'? He never was, of course.) I also saw Myshkin, and once I caught a glimpse of the frightened man in the *Letters From The Underworld . . .* what was his name? But I think the best portrait of all—I mean the silhouette of his personality—is given by the character Sylvia on p. 54 of *Sexus*. I copy it out with a few light cuts (not for four-letter reasons, but because of length) . . .

' . . . You will cause a lot of harm to others in defending yourself from your own fears and doubts. You are not even sure at this moment that you will go back to the woman you love. I have poisoned your mind. You would drop her like that if you were sure that you could do what you wanted without her aid. But you need her and you will call it love. . . . Because the woman can never give you what you want you make yourself out to be a martyr. A woman wants love and you are incapable of giving love. If you were a lower type of man you would be a monster; but you will convert your frustration into something useful. Yes, by all means go on writing. Art can transform the hideous into the beautiful. Better a monstrous book than a monstrous life. If you don't die in the attempt your work might transform you into a sociable, charitable human being. You are big enough not to be satisfied with mere fame, I can see that. Probably when you have lived enough you will discover that there is something beyond what you now call life. You may yet live to live for others. That depends on what use you make of your intelligence, for you are not as intelligent as you think you are. That is your weakness, overweening intellectual pride. . . . You have all the feminine virtues but you are ashamed to acknowledge them to yourself. You think because you are strong sexually that you are a virile man but you are more of a woman than a man. Your sexual virility is only the sign of a higher power which you haven't begun to use. Don't try to prove yourself a man by exploiting your sexual powers. Women are not fooled by that sort of strength and charm. Women, even when they are subjugated mentally, are always master of the situation. A woman may be enslaved sexually and yet dominate the man. You will have a harder time than other men because to dominate another doesn't interest you. You will always be trying to dominate yourself; the woman you love will only be an instrument for you to practise on. . . .'

I wonder if you will think all this nonsense?

Larry.

From Henry Miller

to Lawrence Durrell

Dear Larry,

Your two letters to Fred, of which you so thoughtfully sent me carbons, excite me no end. Not because it's about *me*, but because of the nature of the project. What a task! Of course, you won't really get anywhere, you know. Take that for granted immediately—and you'll travel far and enjoy it.

There are many, many things come to my mind at the outset. Helpful hints and clues, for the most part. Though I trust you understand that I too have difficulty putting my finger on 'it', making the right, eternal statement. But I can offer some correctives and some new tacks, perhaps.

One of the first things that hits me between the eyes is this effort you are making to discover the 'intention'. You speak of the difficulty of explaining or placing me with the younger generation. And with it you couple this business of morality and iconoclasm. As the recipient of thousands of letters, most of them from young people, I get such a different picture. (Could it be that there is this difference in comprehension between the British and the American youth?) At any rate, the young who write me do 'get' me to an amazing extent. Naturally, they 'identify' with me, particularly those who are trying to express themselves. But how interesting it is that the same situations are at work eternally and eternally molding new artists. One could almost sum it up, like Lawrence, and say our troubles are largely, almost exclusively, societal. The social pattern remains the same, fundamentally, despite all the dazzling changes we have witnessed. It gets more thwarting all the time—for the born individualist. And, as you know, I am interested—like God—only in the individual.

One of the things which irks me most, with the critics, is the statement you throw out—about being unlike myself.

27

This is simply impossible. I don't care who the artist is, if you study him deeply, sincerely, detachedly, you will find that he and his work are one. If it were otherwise the planets would be capable of leaving their orbits. I think your trouble may lie here, that the part of me you don't know from direct experience —I mean the me of youth, of long before we met—you tend to idealize. The man you met in the Villa Seurat was a kind of monster, in a way, in that he was in the process of transformation. He had become partially civilized, so to speak. The tensions had eased up, he could be himself, and his own, natural self was, at the risk of being immodest, what you always sense and respect in me. (To myself I always think I was born 'ultra-civilized'. Another way of saying it, a more invidious way, would of course be to say that I was over-sensitive.) And I suppose it is always the over-sensitive creatures who, if they are bent on surviving, grow the toughest hides. This tough hide revealed itself in my case, more in what I passively permitted to be done for me and to me than by what I did of my own volition—vindictively, outrageously, and so on. The coward in me always concealed himself in that thick armor of dull passivity. I only grew truly sensitive again when I had attained a certain measure of liberation.

I don't want to embark on another autobiographical fragment! Stop me, for God's sake. If I let myself go it is only because with the years I get new visions of myself, new vistas, and their one value to me is that they are more inclusive pictures of the parts that go to make the whole—the enigmatic whole.

Here I disgress a moment to mention a noticeable difference in the reactions of Europeans to my work. Seldom do they, for instance, speak of these 'discrepancies'. Perhaps they have had too much contact with discordant authors all their lives. They seem to realize, without mentioning it, that all the contrarieties of make-up and attitude are the leaven necessary to the making of the bread. When they are shocked, to take another example, it is because of the language itself, what has been done to it and with it by the author, not by the moral or immoral implications of this language. There is a difference, do you see? And when I say shocked, I mean in a healthy, agreeable way. It is an aesthetic shock, if you like, but one which vibrates throughout their whole being.

And here, all the young, and often the old too, are unanimous in writing of the therapeutic value of my work. They were altered. They thank me, bless me, bless me for 'just being', as they often say.

But to come back to 'intentions'. It is almost classic what I have to say on this score. I know it all by heart, and when you read again, if you read with this in mind, you too will see it very clearly.

(Oh, yes, but before I forget—one important thing! Remember always that, with the exception of 'Cancer', I am writing counter-clockwise. My starting-point will be my end point— the arrival in Paris—or, in another way of speaking, the breakthrough. So what I am telling about is the story of a man you never met, never knew; he is mostly of a definite period, from the time he met June (Mona-Mara) until he leaves for Paris. Naturally, some of what he is at the time of writing comes to the fore. Inevitable. But the attempt is—I am talking only of the auto-novels, of course—to be and act the man I was during this seven-year period. From this segment of time I am able to look backward and forward. Very much as our own time is described—the Janus period, the turning-point, where both avenues become clear and recognizable—at least to those who see and think. Oof!)

I wanted so much, so much, to be a writer (maybe not to write so much as to *be* a writer). And I doubt that I ever would have become one had it not been for the tragedy with June. Even then, even when I knew I would and could, my intention was to do nothing more than tell the story of those years with her, what it had done to me, to my soul, if you like. Because it was the damage to the soul, I must tell you, that was the all. (And I doubt if I have made that at all clear in my writings!) And so, on the fateful day, in the Park Department of Queen's County, N.Y. I mapped out the whole autobiographical romance—in one sitting. And I have stuck to it amazingly well, considering the pressures this way and that. (The hardest part is coming—*Nexus*—where I must reveal myself for what I was—something less than zero, something worse than the lowest knave.)

With June I could not begin this magnum opus which, as you know, I thought would be just one enormous, endless tome —perhaps bigger than the Bible. My suffering was so great— and my ego too, no doubt—that I imagined it needed a canvas of that scope.

Note: *My* suffering I say. For *then* I was concerned with what had been done *to me*. As I wrote, of course, I began to perceive that what I had done to others was far more heinous. Whoever greatly suffers must be, I suppose, a sublime combination of sadist and masochist. Fred easily perceived the masochist that I was. But neither you nor he see so easily the sadist. Fred has touched on it in a subtly diabolical way—really too exalted to suit my case, I think. It was plainer, coarser than that. (But here you are up against the dilemma of not being privy to the facts of my life; it is my word as a man and a writer, against the apperceptions of readers and critics and psychologists. I admit that I have the power to warp what I honestly think may be the truth about my thoughts and actions. But I do believe I am nearer the mark than the outsider.)

So, as you hint, I coined this word Truth. The key to my whole work to be the utter truth. And, as you realize, I found it easier to give the truth about the ugly side of my nature than the good. The good in me I only know as it is reflected back to me in the eyes and voices of those I talk to.

Whether I *then* knew what later I have come to know absolutely is a question, namely—the words of Jesus, that the truth shall set ye free. If I had only set myself to tell the truth about myself, that would have been fine. But I also wanted to tell the truth about others, about the world. And that's the greatest snare of all: it sets you above the others if not precisely above the world. Time and again I try to cut myself down. You all know how I rant and rave. There's always some truth in these outbursts, to be sure, but how caricatural!

Yet I do feel that truth is linked to violence. Truth is the naked sword; it cuts clean through. And what is it we are fighting, who love truth so much? The lie of the world. A perpetual lie. But I'm going off again . . .

Let me tell you something more simple and yet revealing. I said I wanted nothing more of God than the power to write. Yes, this began in my late teens, I imagine. In my early twenties, confined to my father's shop, a slave to the most idiotic kind of routine imaginable, I broke out—inside. Inwardly I was a perpetual volcano. I will never forget the walks to and from my father's shop every day: the tremendous dialogues I had with my 'characters', the scenes I portrayed, and so on. And never a line of any of this ever put to paper. Where would you begin if you were a smothered volcano?

And then, after the first attempt at a book—when with the Western Union and married to that woman B——, my first wife—I dream of making my entry into the lists—by the back door. To write something that will sell, that people will read, that will permit me to say—'There is my name signed to it, you see.' Proof.

And then the break, thanks to June, the plunge. And I am free, spoon-fed, have leisure, paper, everything, but can't do it. Oh yes, I do write, but how painfully, and how poorly, how imitatively. And then when June left for France with her friend Jean Kronski, then I broke, then I mapped out my whole career. And even then, think of it, even after leaving for France, three years later, I still do not begin that great work. I write *Tropic of Cancer*, which was not in the schema—but of the moment. I suppose one could liken it to the volcano's eruption, to the breaking of the crust. (Only, let me say it as knows, it was such a feeble eruption compared to those imaginary street-walking ones I had every day, inwardly, walking to and from my father's shop!)

How well I know the tremendous décalage between what one wishes to do and what one does! Nowhere in my work have I come anywhere near to expressing what I meant to express. Now, if you can believe this, and I am sure you must because you must also suffer it, then imagine what sort of beast it is that a woman, any woman, has to live with who marries a writer. Imagine what happens to one who never says all, never does all, who smiles and nods his head in that civilized way and is all the while a raging bull. Well, what happens is that either the writer gains the upper hand eventually, or the man. One or the other must take the lead. My effort has been to give the lead to the man in me. (With what success others know best.) But there is no war involved, you must understand. It is rather a matter of leaning more this way than that, of shifting the emphasis, and so forth.

And I do not want to be a saint! Morality, in fact, drops out of the picture. Maybe the writer will drop out too. Or the man. Never the ego, rest assured. Nor do I give a damn about that.

I certainly do not hope to alter the world. Perhaps I can put it best by saying that I hope to alter my own vision of the world. I want to be more and more myself, ridiculous as that may sound.

Where the writing is concerned, I did nothing consciously. I followed my nose. I blew with every wind. I accepted every influence, good or bad. My intention, was there—as I said, merely to write. Or, *to be a writer*, more justly. Well, I've been it. Now I just want—to be. Remember, I beg you, that this infinitive is 'transitive' in Chinese. And I am nothing if not Chinese.

Does this help? If not, walk on—and over me.

Henry.

Next day—April 2nd.

It's pouring and I feel like saying a bit more. . . .

Those fan letters I spoke of. If someone had the courage to publish these, volume after volume, what a broadside that would be. And how revealing! Here are the books which readers say have influenced them, enlarged their outlook on life, altered their being: The Colossus, Capricorn, Cancer, Wisdom of the Heart—primarily. But there are others in which *I* believe I have given most revelatory passages: the Books in my Life, Rimbaud, the Hamlet letters, even Aller-Retour New York. And in The Brooklyn Bridge—where is that?—I am astounded each time I read it by what I have said 'unknowingly'.

There is another too, quite important: 'The World of Sex'. Noone has ever written me *against* this book—or the Colossus. Curious, what! When I speak of Books in my Life and the Rimbaud, I mean the passages about youth, as in the Rider Haggard chapter and the last chapter, called 'The Theatre', where I dwell on the Xerxes society days.

Myself I like Plexus very much, not for the revelatory this time, but for the fantastic bits—about Stanley, about Mimi Aguglia and what follows, about John Brown, and Picodiribibi. Enough. . . .

What I can never write enough about are the 'influences'— both men, haphazard meetings, books, places. Places have affected me as much or more than people, I think. (I find it the same with you here.) Think of my repeated journeys to Toulouse, or of the returns to the old neighbourhood (the 14th Ward), or to the places where as a boy I spent my summer vacations, or to the regions in America where I dreamed things my own way, only to find them so otherwise. Strange that I never think of the afterlife this way! Dear old Devachan, which Fred and Edgar and I spoke of so often. All I see there is a breathing spell, another 'open' womb, so to speak, where all the senses and the intellect are intensified, clarified, unobstructed—and one learns just by looking, looking back at one's meagre, pitiable self in action.

But this business of youth—rebellion, longing for freedom— and the business of vision are two very cardinal points in my orientation. At sixty-six I am more rebellious than I was at 16. Now I *know* the whole structure must topple, must be razed. Now I am positive that youth is right,—or the child in its innocence. Nothing less will do, will satisfy. The only purpose of knowledge must be certitude, and this certitude must be established through purity, through innocence. Fred can tell you of the unknown man from Pekin who hangs above my doorway here. When I look at him I know he knows and is all that I expect a human being to be. (The photo of him is on the back of the Penguin edition of the Colossus. Study it. That is the person or being I would like to be, if I wanted to be someone else than I am.)

c

Influences . . . It should have been an eye-opener for you to read that chapter in the Books in My Life. At various times you have credited me with a live interest in certain writers and thinkers, who to tell the truth, were only passing fancies. My loyalty and adoration have been constant—for the same men, all throughout my life: Whitman, Emerson, Thoreau, Rabelais, above all. I still think that no one has ever had a larger, freer, healthier view of man and his universe than Walt Whitman. And the passage from one of his prose works which I cited in my essay on him (originally published in some French anthology, now in English in the Colorado Review) comes close to expressing my own view of how man may live and function in this world with joy and meaning and purpose. (Look it up!)

And there was always Lao-tse, even before I had read him. He stands there, at the back of one's head, like the great Ancestor. Old Adam Cadmus. ('What's all the fuss about? Take it easy! Sit down, get quiet, don't think. . . . *Think*!') And from him the line of Zen masters, which I only got wise to from Villa Seurat days on. 'When you walk, walk; when you sit, sit; but don't wobble!'

But noone, it seems to me, can honestly put his finger on the real and vital influences which affected his course. That's why I mentioned, along with books and people, trivial things as well—things, happenings (little events), dreams, reveries, places.

In a book, for example,—I say in a book and not *the* book, or a certain book—there are lines, just lines page so and so, top left, that stand out like mountain peaks—and they made you what you have become. No one else but you could respond to those lines. They were written *for* you. Just as everything else which happens to you was intended *for* you, and never mistake it. Particularly the bad things.

(And this reminds me to say again that perhaps one reason why I have stressed so much the immoral, the wicked, the ugly, the cruel in my work is because I wanted others to know how valuable these are, how equally if not more important than the good things. Always underneath, you see, this idea of 'acceptance'—which is Whitman's great theme, his contribution.)

And then there is this curious business about Knut Hamsun.

The one writer I started out to write like, to be like. How much time and thought I have given to that man's work—in the past. How I struggled to phrase my thoughts as he did. And without the least success. No one has ever remarked on it, after reading me. How do you explain that? When you look at early Picassos, early Gauguins, early Van Goghs, you can very easily trace their influences, their idols. They did not begin as Picasso, as Gauguin, as Van Gogh. I sometimes think of those two novels I wrote before going to Paris: what was I, who was I then? I have borrowed these scripts from the Library time and again, but I am never able to read them.

And then I must say another thing—perhaps it bears on the foregoing, perhaps not. . . . The other day I began reading *A Glastonbury Romance* by John Cowper Powys. My head began bursting as I read. No, I said to myself, it is impossible that any man can put all this—so much!—down on paper. It is super-human. And what was it stirred me so? A description of a man and a woman in a boat floating down-stream. (I thought of that marvellous Japanese expression employed, I believe, to describe a certain genre of painting; 'This floating world'.) Old John had caught the world by the throat. And lovingly and surely he squeezed every bit of beauty, of meaning, of purposeless purpose out of it in a few pages. Utterly phenomenal.

And old Friar John, as he calls himself, was one of my first living idols. I a lad then of about 25 and he in his forties. The first man I beheld who was possessed by his daemon. Talk such as I have never heard again in my life. Inspired talk. And now at 80 he is still inspired, still writing masterpieces, still filled with the joie de vivre, the élan vital. You mentioned Chuang-Tzu. He was old John's great favourite. I too loved him better than Lao-tse, I must admit.

You mentioned Otto Rank. Yes, dear Otto too. But then, you know, after a time it palled. *What*? This seeking for meaning in everything. So Germanic! This urge to make everything profound. What nonsense! If only they could also make everything unimportant at the same time!

Ah yes, only a few years ago it was that I stumbled on Hesse's

Siddhartha. Nothing since the Tao Teh Ching meant so much to me. A short book, a simple book, profound perhaps, but carrying with it the smile of that old man from Pekin over my doorway. The smile of 'above the battle'. Overcoming the world. And thus finding it. For we must not only be in it and above it, but of it too. To love it for what it is—how difficult! And yet it's the first, the only task. Evade it, and you are lost. Lose yourself in it and you are free.

How I love the dying words of St. Thomas Aquinas: 'All that I have written now seems so much straw!' Finally he saw. At the very last minute. He knew—and he was wordless. If it takes ninety-nine years to attain such a moment, fine! We are all bound up with the Creator in the process. The ninety-eight years are so much sticks of wood to kindle the fire. It's the fire that counts.

To come back . . . The child is alive with this fire, and we, the adults, smother it as best we can. When we cease throwing the wood of ignorance on the fire, it bursts forth again. Experience is an unlearning, an undoing. We must start from the beginning, not on the backs of dinosaurs—culture, that is, in all its guises. 'Lime twigs and treachery'—that will be the title of a forthcoming book if I can ever get down to it. The title is borrowed from one of Brahms' 'Waltz Songs', so help me God, What matter?

And now to close with a passage from *Les Provinces de France*, which I look at once in a while, nostalgically:

'L'herbe n'a jamais repoussé sous les pas du cheval de Simon de Montfort, de sinistre mémoire . . . Le talent n'a jamais refleuri, le génie est mort à jamais. Il ne reste aux Languedociens, avec leur austère protestantisme, que des grâces superficielles. Race à fleur de peau . . .

'En somme, pour qui pense que la Haute Garonne est bien près d'être pyrénéenne, que l'Aude pourrait faire partie du Roussillon, Nïmes apparaït comme la véritable capitale du Languedoc, dans le Gard où tout est sobre et ordonné, où rien n'est plantureux, abondant, insolent, mais où tout . . . (je cherche le mot qui convient), ou tout est *muscat*.'

Allez voir Joseph Delteil à Montpellier un de ces jours. Ça

vous fera, vous et Claude, du bien. Il peut vous parler des Albigeois—et mille autres choses, comme St. François, par exemple, ou le cimetière à Sete et l'esprit qui y trouve son sommeil tranquille, Paul Valéry. Salut a Fréderic Temple et au Pont du Gard. Je l'ai vu pour la première fois en 1928 quand June et moi ont fait un tour de France avec bicyclettes. Je n'oublierai jamais ma première vue de la Méditerranée, des oliviers, des vignes, de tout un pays ensoleillé et sec et brillant comme une gemme.

Ta-ta! Assez pour une séance.

Henry.

From Henry Miller

to Alfred Perlès

Dear Fred,

Just got your two letters to Larry and once again I can't restrain myself . . . must add a few words. Of course I wept a little—*le vieux pleurnicheur!*—but then I began laughing and I couldn't stop. (Haven't laughed so hard since you left four years ago!) That same mail brought me the two volumes of *Sexus* (in Swedish). Thinking to restore my equanimity, I opened volume one at random, and then I began really laughing like a madman. Here is what I read—wouldn't it make any man laugh his guts out? What a language!

' "Langa hit den bara," sa jag, och tog honom i armen. "Det ar ingenting att sta och dividera om nu." Vi gick ut i hallen och han stack at mig en sedel. Just som vi var pa vag mot dorren kom Irene ut ur badrummet. "Ni tanker val inte ga?" . . . "Jo, han maste skynda sig ivag nu," sa Ulric, men han har lovat att jomma tillbaka senare.'

(Sweden's greatest poet is now on his way to see me, dispatched by the Cultural attaché in Washington. Must be serious when he comes.)

How curious it is, this business of who owes whom, of master and disciple. When I added that final letter, from Spain, to our 'Aller-Retour' correspondence, I tried so hard to explain that it is I who am indebted—to *you*. Do you want to know the secret, or the test of 'masterhood'? The master is he who can make you laugh the hardest and longest. And Joey, that's you! Somewhere there is mention of Rabelais's humor. Yes, there were two great things (aside from the 'word lists') which I got from Master Rabelais: one, laughter, two, the holy bottle. The one who understands the meaning of the holy bottle always reaches you—and cures you—through laughter. (And in my peculiar way I connect such austere and democratic figures as

Emerson and Whitman with Rabelais because all three knew, as few men do, the origin and the meaning of creation—or creativity. In Zen all this is resynchronized and reoriented: the humor, the leveling off, the annihilation of Buddhas, masters, geniuses, and the sure knowledge that creation is endless and inexhaustible.)

When I hear the word Culture I reach for my revolver. Remember that? So, too, when I hear the word Genius. I never felt I had genius, even if I boasted about it in my writings. I always feel that I am 'just a Brooklyn boy.' (And here I urge you to read again Emil Schnellock's and Knut Merrild's contributions to *The Happy Rock*.) They came very close to sizing me up; they had that human approach which you so rightly stress.

But to return for one moment to the master-disciple business. Each of us is both at once, is he not? Even Jesus and Buddha were disciples—of whom or what we do not know. The only master is life. To be just a master is to be static, dead. As long as we are alive we are growing, stretching out our hands towards God . . . any God. And God is reaching down to us. No end, no conclusion, no completion. Perpetual becoming.

And so pertinent to all the foregoing is what you say about spirit and flesh. They are one, of course. And suddenly I saw myself as the 'earnest young man,' the youth with a book under his arm, wherever he went. And how is it all the critics, and even my good friends sometimes, forget what I have told about so often—my efforts to find a God, a religion, a belief, a way of life. At a very early age too. New Thought, Ethical Culture, Theosophy, the Bahai Movement . . . what didn't I look into? And that Evangelist, Benjamin Fay Mills, whom Bob Challacombe introduced me to! How much I owe that man! How much I still revere him! Don't you know that story of how I heard him lecture and, moved to the guts, I went down to speak to him (from the gallery) and I said, as only an 'innocent' could: 'Dear Sir, I believe that I am one who should hear your (private) lectures. I know what you are thinking about. Couldn't you let me do something for you to pay for those lectures?' (It cost about a hundred dollars for the series.) And

I shall never forget the look he gave me, a long, down-slanting look with piercing gimlet eyes, like those of a mage or an old witch. And after reading my very soul, it seemed, he said, breaking into a smile: 'Of course you are the man! Certainly you shall hear the lectures.' And then he suggested that I pay for them by passing the salver around (for money) after his public lectures. Which I did. (Can you picture me doing that?)

There's another point in your letter which interests me— that of the seemingly perpetual *décalage* between the writer and his work, the man and his product. I can't see why people dwell on this as much as they do, finding disappointment in either the man or his work. In life, it seems so obvious, man has a more limited scope to the play of his many-faceted being. There are exceptions to be sure—in the hero type—men like Alexander, Caesar, Napoleon, artists in action. But how many writers can do or be what they do and are through their characters in books? Exceptions again—Voltaire, Casanova, Cendrars, for example. But usually where life is exalted the art suffers, and vice versa.

And this brings me, perhaps for the nth time, to the business which you all seem agreed upon and wish to explain away: the slag. Nice that image of the volcano. Flattering. But let me give you a look again at myself as I see myself, that is, see myself writing. What is my weakness? The desire to devour all. Or, and from a Zen view not such a weakness either, the desire to imitate life. Not record or present life, but imitate it, in short, make books live. All this leading to that point I began to make in my writings, and which bothers writers no end, that the highest art is the art of living, that writing is but a prelude or form of initiation for this purpose. From this standpoint most every writer is consequently a rank failure. The fear which writers or artists in general have when confronted with such an issue is that art would disappear. Dear Art! As if anything could destroy it. How do you destroy the cornerstone of life? Why worry? True, we may eliminate the hot-house geniuses— but on the other hand we might, once again, endow everything we see, do, touch or think about with art. We may all become, or re-become, artists! There is the kind of immolation (of the artist) I believe in.

But even from a limited, academic, hide-bound point of view, the traditional art view, how silly it is for critics to be disturbed about slag, excrescences, drift and scoriae. How little they understand the role or the value of the so-called non-essential, the commonplace, the ugly, the inartistic. Their desire for perfection is so similar to that false religious attitude which desires only the good. You may think I am trying to justify my weakness. No, I am trying to tell you that I learned as much, or more, from the bad, the wrong, the slipshod, the evil, the misfit, and so on, than the other way round. When we speak of a person getting to grips with himself, accepting himself for what he is, we do not simply mean that he admits and recognizes his weaknesses but that he also discovers how important they were in his evolution. Asked how long a man's legs should be, Lincoln replied: 'Just long enough to reach from his waist to the ground.'

And then there's another thing about the drift and slag . . . have you ever noticed how, in life, there come these dull, dull moments when everything drags, everything seems futile, and you grow into a sort of vegetable . . . and just when you have reached the nadir, so to speak, of your being, there comes an awakening from deep down, like a flower opening its petals, and little by little, as if there were chinks in your armor, the light seeps in, stirs you gently back to life and awareness. But that vegetable pause or break was necessary; without it there would be no wonderful return. I say 'wonderful' return to distinguish it from the usual returns which occur more frequently—because admit it or not, we are continually on the verge of falling asleep (mentally, morally, spiritually). In this wonderful return you dimly, unconsciously perhaps, realize the significance of that word gamut, that you or 'it' (again) are strung along a gamut of being which is not human only but animal, vegetable, mineral. These fantasies which I indulge in occasionally (in the books), are not some of them distinctly mineral, others vegetable, and so on? Of course, I know you and Larry are not objecting to the 'fantasies' or even the less valid excursi, but rather to a sort of everyday writing or thinking which is supposedly a betrayal of the artist in oneself. Don't worry about it!

Don't explain it! Think of an adorable 'haiku.' (Here a crazy thought intrudes. No one of the faithful disciples ever spoke of Jesus farting or even blowing his nose. But he must have, what! Would it have been inartistic, sacrilegious, irreverent to introduce such a note? There are many still who can't excuse him, who refuse to believe, that in his agony on the cross he cried out: 'O Lord, why hast thou forsaken me!' A saviour shouldn't have spoken such words, they will tell you. And yet it is this, just this piece of weakness, of doubt, of complaint, that is the most human thing about Jesus, that keeps him linked to us human-all-too-human trash).

And now a final word about 'intentions.' I think you are quite right in thinking that my intentions do not matter much. Or did not. Man proposes, God disposes. How often I think of Rabelais who, while working for the printer, decided that he could write just as lusty and humorous works as those he was printing. And he did. *But* . . . then he got caught in his own machinery, as it were. He got terribly serious. He employed his Gargantuan humor to awaken us to greater things. He had intended to do something with his left hand, merely. ("The left hand is the dreamer.") He got caught. He had stirred the muddy waters of his own being. He awoke the artist in him, the creator, the imaginator. And so, true to his lights, poor devil that he is, he is driven from pillar to post, always trying to save his skin—and tell the truth.

And now an 'excursus' . . . The other day I meant to sit down and tell you lads of the wonderful remembrance which came to me. Suddenly one morning I fell to thinking of that trip abroad in 1953, with Eve. And suddenly it occurred to me how blessed was that trip from one aspect alone: my visits to the homes of certain celebrated men. What a list it is! Rabelais, da Vinci, Moses Maimonides, El Greco, Ruysbroeck the Admirable, Shakespeare, Proust, Van Eyck . . . And throw in the Cathedral of Chartres and the Mosque of Cordova. Each home, each countryside, each atmosphere was so very different. I say 'home.' Not always. Da Vinci, for example—the Château at Amboise, where he died. Proust, the countryside made famous in the Côté de Guermantes. Van Eyck, the famous triptych in the Cathedral at Ghent. But the home of Rabelais, yes! The most idyllic countryside, as I glimpsed it from the window where his cradle once stood, I have ever laid eyes on. Across it had marched Joan of Arc, to meet the king. El Greco, on the other hand—I am thinking of Toledo—inhabited a doll's house. All miniature rooms, and an alcove, off the dining room, where the musicians played for him as he ate. Around and about his dwelling the strongest, grimmest, severest city I have ever stepped into: Toledo. Rock and torture. Superstition, pomp, cruelty, ignorance, intolerance. And then the cloister in the forest outside Brussels, where Ruysbroeck lived. How serene, how ordered, how noble and silent and grave! A forest entirely of beeches, if I remember right. And then Bruges. The most alive of the dead. Saying to myself—I would get lost every time I took a walk—what a pity I never lived here. Here I could have written such a different book!

I forgot Cervantes . . . Yes, through his country too we passed. Got off to look at the no longer existing windmills. Think of it, though. Oh yes, and even more important than all these . . . With Delteil we made a détour coming out of Spain and passed by that mountain where the last of the Albigensians had been walled in.

And another name still: Nostradamus. Not only my talks with the French doctor, but my talks with the man and wife who maintained Michel Simon's home in La Ciotât. They came from Nostradamus' country. They communed with Petrarch.

I'll reel them off again, and twenty-one salutes to Waremme (of 'The Maurizius Case'): Nostradamus, Cervantes, Ruysbroeck, El Greco, Rabelais, Proust, da Vinci, Moses Maimonides, Shakespeare—and Old Friar John (Powys). And just a stone's throw from Glastonbury—and all Arthur's great realm around us . . . 'the matter of Britain,' as they say . . . Joey, I must get back to work. So long. Tootle—oo.

Henry.

From Alfred Perlès

to Lawrence Durrell

Dear Larry,

It's actually your turn but it doesn't seem to matter much now. We've started out on this correspondence in a rather leisurely manner, as though there were no hurry of coming to the point, namely to reveal Henry's intentions to those of his readers, admirers and detractors alike, who haven't been able to get hold of his essential books and therefore can't make up their minds about him one way or the other. And all we have achieved (unless we carry this to unconscionable lengths) was to arouse the subject of our epistolary exchanges to the point of butting in on our correspondence with a premature but final *mise au point* which, in a way, condemns our endeavour to a sort of *fausse-couche*. Perhaps it would have been wiser to conclude our own little investigation and listen to what he has to say about it afterwards instead of practically inviting his unrestrained comments midstream, as it were. That should teach us a lesson: we'll know better the next time—if there is a next time.

But maybe everything's for the best: for, as Henry submits, haven't we, after all, embarked on a rather hopeless task? Could we really have thrown a new light on him? It is doubtful. The effective manner with which he now shuts us up is like the tweaking of the pupils' noses by the Zen master, no? And yet we have achieved something: by provoking him we have succeeded in making him come out in the open, take the wind out of our sails, and settle with his customary ebullience the whole matter himself. We could now call it a day, consider our faces saved, pass on the result of our aborted enquiry to the reader, and then revert to other, less controversial activities.

Only I, for one, am not quite satisfied. It seems to me that Henry's *mise au point* calls for another *mise au point* of our own.

Not that Henry doesn't hit the nail on the head, as usual, but one or two things remain to be said. He doesn't claim to be able to put the finger on the enigma of his own personality and only insists on coming nearer the mark than the outsider. Which is fair enough: no human being, considered as a self-contained entity, can wholly be understood by another, regardless of love, sympathy and affinity. The outsider can observe and analyse, but observation and analysis at best yield circumstantial evidence, not true knowledge. True knowledge of ourselves can only be sensed by ourselves—only sensed, not communicated: because the enigma that *justifies* our personality always remains veiled, secret—if for no other reason, then because it is meant to be.

Frankly, the more I think about what we set out to do, especially in view of Henry's vehement reaction to our initial effort, the more I am convinced that we could not have added one iota of verisimilitude to the picture of the man we were trying to depict. Reading over our short-lived correspondence, it seems to me that we were off the track right from the start: we were both pulling in different directions, not coming to grips: like boxers closing in on each other to avoid a k.o. blow, with no referee to pull us apart. It suited me fine, for I don't really like blows. And that's why I'm not altogether displeased that Henry has stepped into the ring and settled the argument for us. Settled it? Perhaps not quite. Let me give you my reaction to his letters, and you can then have the last word.

To begin with, I fully agree that Henry's letter to you is a gem which could serve as an introduction to his whole work if it weren't for the fact that the letter is as spontaneously desultory as his whole work: as in his books he touches on a variety of subjects, lets them slip by, takes them up again or doesn't, and only those who know the man intuitively, as I believe I do, will be any the wiser. For Henry, and this must be said here and now, lives and writes *au jour le jour*, which is one of his mottos. 'Always Merry and Bright' is another one. I'll come to that presently. Now if the *au-jour-le-jour* attitude, so tempting to him because of his Zen leanings, makes for spontaneity and carefreeness, it also paves the way to a sort of facile *je-m'en-foutisme*. For after all man is not really a lily-in-the-field and can't live like one. I do believe that Henry's 'inspiration' comes straight from the source but he does nothing to *refine* it: he is crude oil, made by God Himself, but it won't take him on stratospheric flights, so to speak. He picks up anything, casts aside anything, not excluding himself. He can do so with impunity because he *is* a genius, a fact upon which we're all agreed, even though he turns his nose up at the word and reaches for his revolver. Fine, let him. If such an outside organization as the American Academy of Arts and Letters can elect him as a member, we have a perfect right to award him *d'office* the title of genius. In the face of his protest I will concur to this degree: he may not *have* genius but he *is* one; there's a subtle distinction to be made. Apart from his narrative and descriptive writing, which has a highly original flavour of its own and upon which his fame as a writer will eventually no doubt rest, he has not said or written a word that hasn't been said or written before, sometimes better, sometimes not so well. What he advocates is as old as thinking man; his 'message' as ancient as the Hermetic Brotherhood. I am not saying this in an attempt to diminish his value—far from it; for although he has not invented the *fil à couper le beurre* he has done more and better than just introducing us to a new way of life, a new philosophy, a new religion. And all owing to his curious digestion!

He insists on having read a great deal (much more than the books in his life) . . . from Buddha to Jesus Christ (neither of whom has written a word), from the Upanishads to Keyserling and Spengler, via Nostradamus, the 18th-century philosophers and the 19th and 20th century psycho-analysts. And whatever he reads is later resuscitated in the most astounding guises under the chemical action of his mysterious digestive system. But he doesn't let it rest at that. As a friend who has known him for the last thirty years I can affirm that he actually does as he preaches, even though what he preaches isn't strictly speaking his own formula but a fantastically digested *pot-pourri* of the literary-philosophic world literature which any half-educated person knows.

Henry is no Plato, no Lao-Tzu, no Spinoza, no Nietzsche, no

Freud—he is better: he is himself, which very few human beings are able to be, and that's why I maintain that he is a genius though he may not have any genius. And if he has never uttered anything new—perhaps because there's nothing new under the sun—he is yet a creator! And one of the most lovable ones. He's a creator in the sense that anything he touches upon, even the oldest most threadbare idea, suddenly becomes new, like a wall that has just been distempered. Under the enigmatic mental processes of his digestion there invariably happens the miracle of freshness, and there can never be the slightest objection to his splendidly naïve emphasis on the obvious: every truism assumes a refreshingly, caricaturally novel aspect as it passes through the sieve of his mind, the astonishingly cockeyed logic of the artist to which there is no answer. Everything he looks upon with his innocent child's eyes, which 67 years have not succeeded in tarnishing, assumes a different shape, a different meaning, a different purpose, a different truth even. And it's no use saying that he sees things that aren't there, for if they weren't there he couldn't see them and pick them out as essential. The 'farting Christ' in his letter to me is characteristic in this respect but no one but Henry could think or say such a thing without seeming incongruous or blasphemous.

God only knows what he made of the writers who so *influenced* him: Dostoevsky, Knut Hamsun, Rabelais, Voltaire, Thoreau, Emerson, Whitman, Lawrence, Proust, John Cowper Powys, Rider Haggard, Blaise Cendrars *et alii*. Whatever he reads becomes automatically distorted, he ingurgitates one thing and excretes another, and it is a safe bet to say that the influence of those writers *on him* is not the least implicit in their works. But a minor detail like that doesn't worry Henry: he takes hold of his haul, swallows it without chewing like a phenomenal shark, lets it pass through his digestion, then, adding himself to the booty, presents us with a novel interpretation of things. If that is not genius, I ask you, what is?

His writing has often been criticised, even by his closest associates and friends, but that is quibbling. When he does pour himself out recklessly, when his pages begin to glimmer and grow incandescent with gems of all colours and magnitudes, as in parts of the *Tropics*, *Black Spring*, the *World of Sex*, *Colossus of Maroussi*, etc., etc., aren't we all overwhelmed and happy? What matter that his writing is uneven, interspersed with platitudes and long passages of downright bad writing as in *Sexus* and *Plexus*, in the Rimbaud book and his latest *Big Sur And The Oranges of Hieronymus Bosch*? Who are we—who, above all, am I—to throw the first stone at him? He says he always wanted to *be* a writer rather than write. How well I can understand this paradox, this apparent incongruity. Well, Henry *is* a writer, isn't he? He is a writer even when he doesn't write, when he sits or talks or eats or dreams or just breathes. If *being* a writer was his ambition he certainly has achieved it.

But as a writer he has always been the *amateur* (in the etymological sense of the term); a vocational writer, yes, and also a professional writer, but one of the most unprofessionally professional writers that ever lived! He never writes except up to his highest level, and sustains it. The fact that the level is not always even, is irrelevant. Naturally there are ups and downs; like the earth he is only round when seen from the distance; it's only when one comes closer that one distinguishes the unevenness of the surface, the lowlands, the valleys, the deep crevasses as well as the Himalayas. Henry the artist, whom I cannot isolate from the man, is as round as the earth (but not rounder), as hot as the sun, as cold as the moon. And I don't care if he isn't always a *good* writer—a writer he *is*!

And anyhow, how could a writer of Henry's output be always equally good? It wouldn't be a miracle, it would be monstrous! The greatest spirits of all times have never written a line, no doubt because they *knew* that writing is essentially useless. As for us, we're attached to literature and we love writing but we must not forget that writing is a surrogate, a substitute for something else, something more important. Why, I wonder, hasn't Socrates ever written a word? Somehow I can't believe he was simply relying on Plato to do the job for him. And none of Henry's great Chinese masters was particularly prolific. I doubt that Lao-Tzu's writing is larger (in size) than *Aller-Retour New York*. Idem Confucius. Idem Mencius. When a man grows over a certain stature he stops writing altogether.

Henry is perfectly aware of this and says himself that 'the highest art is the art of living, that writing is but a prelude or form of initiation for this purpose.' But why single out writing? All the roads lead to Rome and the 'high art of living' can be mastered in many different ways from writing. It would be more à propos to say that living in the highest sense is impossible for the man who is devoured by *any* passion, be it literature or sport, sensuality or greed, money, gluttony, sex, vanity, or even religion. Because passion detracts, and our noblest passions are but prefatory to the Life with the capital L, which must needs be static, still and pure. Isn't that why Buddha is always depicted in motionlessness, sometimes with a flower in his hand?

But thank God, Larry, we aren't there yet. And thank God, Henry isn't either. Or we'd never catch up with him. I don't mind him being a genius, but a Buddha—no! So let me wind up this letter with my image of Henry as of *now*, not as he will be in ten trillion light years.

Au jour le jour. You can't have the cake and eat it. Our good friend Henry now complains about the *décalage* between what one wishes to do and what one does. And goes on telling you in his gem of a letter that nowhere in his work has he come anywhere near to expressing what he meant to express. Great wonder, this, no? Personally I'm rather pleased with that *décalage*. There's no telling what his work might have turned out to be had he expressed exactly what he meant to express. Of course it *might* have been more wonderful than the best he actually wrote: and again it might have been infinitely inferior to his worst writing. All speculation on these lines is futile and I hold that a bird in the hand is better than two in the bush. But this *décalage* he talks about is a fact and, in his case, probably wider than with most writers. Offhand I should say that in the writings of, say Proust, the discrepancy between intention and expression is marked to a lesser degree. And this discrepancy would be smaller still with certain long-winded utterly boring pseudo-philosophers (no need to mention names) who painstakingly adhere to some dry preconceived synopsis and plod along over the years like local acting unpaid lance corporals of letters! But Henry who works and lives *au jour le jour* cannot be

D

expected to stick to five or ten-year plans, can he? His *décalage* is conditioned and willed by life itself—not the static, serene Buddha Life but the flux and reflux of ordinary every-day life. Just imagine for a moment that Henry had stuck to his original schedule and given us the June-Mona-Mara version at Bible length and thrown out *Cancer* which, as he now says, wasn't on the menu at all and is but 'a feeble eruption of the crust.' Fortunately there never was any danger of such a thing happening: Henry, the *au-jour-le-jour viveur* and artist had too much intuitive sense to adhere to a premeditated plan or synopsis, thank God once more! Also for his formlessness, chaotic subject matter, treatment and language of his good *and* bad books!

Always Merry and Bright! He loves suffering and he loves laughter. Here I must admit that I always was a little shocked by the evident delight with which he would talk and write about his suffering. To me it seemed indecent! Not the actual suffering but the relish with which he dwelled on it, asking for more, as it were. As you must know, I'm not precisely thick-skinned myself, and it goes without saying that any sensitive person suffers. But I should never dream of displaying the welts openly, baring the scars and cicatrices of hurts ancient and fresh. One's suffering is only of value if it turns into experience, mellows the man and renders him more human, and in the case of a writer should be *implicit* in his work, not shouted out as by a town-crier. With shameless enthusiasm, as Henry does it. Perhaps I'm a bit too *faisandé* to make a song and dance about my suffering; but Henry goes to the other extreme, almost turns into a Plymouth Brother in his delight of the hurts inflicted on him by the world and by himself. He knows no restraint in this respect and it is this I find shocking! Like bad table manners: belching at a delicious banquet—not once or twice surreptitiously but belching all the time. Suffering is a private affair—perhaps our only private affair—and no one should be admitted to the spectacle: it must be done in silence, in agony, but gracefully. But Henry can't be quiet about it, he must shout it all over the roof-tops and is only satisfied if everybody within earshot can hear him. Perhaps you will agree with me that Henry's suffering is infinitely more poignant and heart-rending when at rare moments, as for example in *The Smile at the Foot of the Ladder*, he succeeds in harnessing it by implication to the story he has to tell.

And what I've just said about suffering goes for laughter as well. *Always Merry and Bright!* Have you ever come across the type of joke-telling bore who keeps priding himself on his 'sense of humour'? Of course you have. And of course there isn't a grain of humour in him! Humour is in many respects like suffering—a thing the sensitive person is endowed with by the gods, perhaps as an antidote to his suffering. It has often been observed that the really great humorist is sad, but it isn't the humour that makes him sad but rather his suffering which his sense of humour is intended to alleviate. And if I may momentarily come out of my shell I might say that my faculty of making Henry laugh, often to the point of tears as he keeps assuring me, is entirely due to my own suffering. *Voilà.* I am speaking of *humour*, not wit, which is a different thing altogether. Humour come from the heart, wit from the mind: humour is soothing, wit often acid: humour scratches the itch of the inner man, wit is directed *against* somebody or something. Being able to make people laugh from the heart rather than the malicious mind, is an undeniable accomplishment. Naturally, laughter goes with weeping, the good old dichotomy again, and that's where Henry comes in, *le vieux pleurnicheur*, as I once referred to him in a book, a word which so pleased him he's never quite forgiven me. But laughter, which is supposed to distinguish us from the animals (I wonder if it really does), being the concomitant of suffering, must also be implied rather than bellowed. An odd thing to say to people like you and Henry who can laugh so heartily you almost start a riot in a café or in the street when you let yourselves go. But there you are! I must indeed be too deliciously *faisandé*, too decadently 'cultured' (makes me almost reach for the revolver myself!) to leave this unsaid before vacating the floor for you to say your own valedictory piece . . .

En résumé, there's nothing wrong with Henry. His heart is in the right place and nothing else matters. Makes no difference whether he is a genius or not, a halfwit or a sage, a sadist or a

masochist, a daemon or an angel, or just a Brooklyn boy, as he
keeps telling us. He's probably a little of all that: he is one and
various, as the light, according to whether you get it straight
from the sun or from the spectrum—but what's the point in
looking at the light in a spectrum? That's about all for the
time being, that and *au jour le jour* and Always Merry and
Bright!

Fred.

From Lawrence Durrell

to Alfred Perlès

Dear Joe,

Yes, you are right; time to call a halt. But even if we have failed we have at least provoked the subject's own long letter—probably the most explicit expression of his own aims and intentions he has ever written; the Preface to his collected work, no less. *This*, at any rate, was worth doing.

Driving back to Paris with Nadeau last month, eagerly discussing Henry, and what the old rogue elephant of modern American literature was up to, I told him that *Sexus* had somewhat shell-shocked me, and that in my usual impulsive way I had written off reproachfully to Henry, accusing him of finger-painting in his own excrement rather than producing art. 'These coprolitic Babbits fornicating in their ferro concrete wilderness . . .' He laughed, we both laughed somewhat ruefully. 'Actually so did I' he said. 'And Henry was naturally rather aggrieved about it.' Then he paused, and added: 'But actually once I got over the shock and re-read the book for its virtues I thought to myself that time would prove me wrong.' Petronius, Rabelais . . . did they *shock* their contemporaries? One wonders. I rather suspect that the type of civilisation they catered for was not shockable in our sense. Whatever it was it wasn't a sort of prurio-Moribundia world.

Sometimes great force must be used to drive a wedge into reality; Henry beats with great wings against the blank walls of our *moeurs*, the very quality of his despair giving his work that mad vital quality. What is fine too is his refusal to be an 'intellectual', his determination to remain a Brooklyn Boy. His books may well be the 'proletarian' literature of the future; and if as you say his public is composed of 'ordinary guys' I cannot

think of a healthier influence than his books. For the central
motif (that art is joy, and within the reach of everyone) is something that badly needs emphasising today, as also does the
religious significance of the artistic act.

No, he has retained (as every artist must) an abnormally large
part of his childhood phantasy-life intact—with all its wounds
and ardours and fantastically *unreasonable* demands upon the
world, upon men. He has re-enacted it all as an adult, and then
written it all out, unwittingly providing a catharsis for the
dammed-up phantasy-life of the Anglo-Saxon. He cuts open
the abscesses which so easily form the puritan unconscious.
The pus and blood gushes out. But if any wound remains, it is
clean, and can heal. Fundamentally all this great lavatory
music holds a vital secret—that of psychic growth. The art and
the outrage march hand in hand towards a dimly recognisable
future in which Henry himself—despite every despair—has
never really lost hope.

Perhaps we were wrong to embark on a discussion of 'truth',
in the accepted sense; your kaleidoscope metaphor is probably
the closest we can get. And here I am reminded of an anecdote
which would strike an appropriate note upon which to end this
correspondence.

Coming to the Villa Seurat early one day I found him
scribbling madly on a large sheet of paper; his breakfast was
beside him—it had been pushed aside. 'This morning' he said
gravely, 'as I took the first mouthful of food the thought came
to me: "Whatever happens death will come, sooner or later."
It filled me with a mixture of joy and apprehension. I feel I
have hardly begun to write down all I want to say. I pushed
aside my plate and feverishly, madly started to make some notes
about my life which will be of use to my biographers. Just the
names of places and people and influences—a sort of synoptic
history of my life. I have got so little of the truth on paper as
yet. It makes me wild with impatience.'

Here he dropped his pencil, speared a mouthful of food and
chewed reflectively for a moment. Then he turned back to me
again and a seraphic and mischievous expression came into his
face; the face of a child with a Big Secret. 'And do you know

what?' he said in a low, conspiratorial tone. '*Here and there I'm deliberately putting down a lie—just to throw the bastards off the track, like.*'

That's all for now.

Larry.

From Henry Miller

to Alfred Perlès

Dear Fred,

It's a strange thing but just a few days before I received your Third Letter to Larry I lay awake early one morning asking myself if all these books I have written (about my life, my suffering, my sins) was really as important, as necessary, as I once thought. I was reading them over from beyond the grave, as it were. I wasn't thinking of them critically but rather as one does sometimes with his own life—of what use, of what good, to what end and so on.

And here is the strange conclusion I came up with: that God had answered my prayers and suffered me to become a writer but, as the gods often do when responding to human pleas, my request had been answered only literally. What do I mean? I am not quite sure if I can tell you exactly, but it's something like this. . . . I proved to my satisfaction that, like any other mortal, I too could write. But since I wasn't really meant to be a writer all that was permitted me to give expression to was this business of writing and being a writer; in short, my own private struggles with this problem. My grief, in other words. Out of the lack I made my song. Very much as if a warrior, challenged to mortal combat and having no weapons, must first forge them himself. And in the process, one that takes all his life, the purpose of his labors gets forgotten or sidetracked.

Sometimes I say to myself, quite seriously, I mean: 'when will you begin to write?' Write like other writers do. Like Larry, for instance, who is definitely what is called 'a born writer'. Or, to put it another way, like Larry who has respect and reverence for his tools, his material. What I have done all through my work is to repeat: 'This is the best I can do; take it or leave it.' Or again: 'If it isn't literature, call it what you like. I don't give a damn.' This, I suppose, is the 'je m'en foutisme' you refer to. And there is truth in it.

When I said that I only approximated what I wanted to say in writing I meant that I do understand what writers are about when they undertake to give us a book. And that I too am aware of what I am about during the genesis of a book. But I never seem capable of submitting to the discipline demanded of an author. And you are again right when you speak of this day by day business. I would even stretch it and say hour by hour. My whole life is a kind of sparking activity. I spark, I don't glow steadily, like a sun. Hence my adoration for the sages, the masters, the great teachers of life. In a word, my infatuation with 'serenity'.

It must strike you as quite fatuous, my saying this. Did you ever suspect anything of the sort of me? I seem to hear you laughing, saying to yourself—'he's in another mood to-day.'

But the truth is that from a very early age this thought formed itself and led me to seek out strange individuals, strange books, even strange adventures. When I come into the presence of the serene at heart I am completely myself, thoroughly stilled, at one with the world, and only then living, living in the full sense of the word. All other times, and they may be good, bad or indifferent, I am not myself but another—'l'autre'. Many others. There's no harm in it, to be sure. It may not be in the least injurious—to the psyche or the immortal soul or what have you. But it's in these rare moments that I know that I know, that I feel complete and realized, that I am free of moods, fears and ambitions, and above all, reach beyond happiness.

Maybe I ought to say a word here about being happy, since you mentioned your suffering. You see, I often tell myself that I was born happy. I never had to reach for it, as so many people do. For me it was the natural state. That may explain, in passing, why I have had to taste so much suffering. I am not sure. I don't want to be facile. It's so easy to make explanations—afterwards.

But here is the strange thing . . . I was happy with myself and in myself. It was the others who brought misery and unhappiness into my life. Not only women, though they chiefly, but men too, my friends and comrades; sometimes just 'the world outside', if you know what I mean. And I don't mean the old hackneyed 'weltschmerz'. I mean before and after the weltschmerz period.

Let us put it another way. People gravitate towards happy souls, but in doing so they tend to make the person unhappy. They *need* happiness. Happy people don't need it, they are it. It isn't produced because of this or that, it just is, and they are blessed though they may know it not. In this country of ours everybody wants to be happy and the result is, as you well know, that we are about as miserable a body of people as the earth has ever spawned. And I loathe my countrymen for dwelling on the subject; they make me most unhappy.

I am floundering a bit but bear with me. The three great periods of anguish I went through were, as you know, with the first girl I fell in love with, then the widow, then June. And in all three periods I was inarticulate. What I needed most desperately was voice with which to express my grief and abandonment. That is how I came to write. My thought was simple and direct. My prayer, I should say, for it virtually took that form. 'Give me, O God,' is what I kept saying, 'the power to express this anguish which afflicts me. Let me tell it to the world, for I can't bear to keep it locked in my own breast.'

It was not until I came to the writing of Capricorn that I began this story of my suffering. I quoted Abelard in the frontispiece, you remember. My ego must have been enormous, to compare my suffering with his. But it was sincere, my feeling.

Perhaps the book that I botched the most of all was Black Spring. I was too happy then. Fate had to remind me of my task. You remember the last appearance of June—in Clichy. It was like sobering up after a long drunk. The time had come to put it down.

All during this Paris period prior to tackling Capricorn I had been enjoying, if I might put it that way, the effect of other men's writing. I was open to any and all influences. Especially from the French. I was writing in my head constantly . . . as they might write, I mean. I was a literary man. I might have written books and not the story of my life.

What happened? I suppose you might say that I suffered a kind of dementia. The more I wrote the more I became a human being. The writing may have seemed monstrous (to some), for it was a violation, but I became a more human individual because of it. I was getting the poison out of my system, no doubt. Curiously enough, this poison had a tonic effect for others. It was as if I had given them some kind of immunity.

What was this poison? Not a hatred that I had to work off, for by the time of writing I had no hate for any of my 'characters'. Indeed, I fell in love with many of them, the ones who lent themselves to ridicule and caricature particularly. All the while puffed up, no doubt, by that vanity which writers are plagued with—the belief that they can enter into the heart and soul of their inventions. And while the writer in me revelled at his prowess the human being had to admit more and more to the annihilating truth that no matter how sincerely, how tenderly, how reverently, he approached the character he was writing about, he could never, never capture him, never enter him, never render back what had been created by God alone. In other words, the truth teller, as I always styled myself, came face to face with the fabricator, or the writer.

Is it any wonder that between whiles, between opera, or between sections of any one book, I gave myself up to the wildest dreams? Oscillating always between the desire to be solely an inventor and the hope to become completely a man of truth? And what was I forging all the while in preparation for that mortal combat? The weapons with which to destroy the warrior who would use them. In short, myself.

No wonder I am full of anomalies, both as writer and as human being. Criticism bounces off me, not because I am vain and self-centered, not because I think I am a great writer . . . oh no! Because, my dear fellow, art has been my life-long preoccupation. The word means nothing to me, nor what it is supposed to stand for. Like God. But I am never fooled by men who pretend they cannot get it past their lips. I don't look

for art in art, any more than I look for God in religion. But if
you have prayed earnestly for certain powers you recognize
them when you witness them, even though you yourself may
never have been granted these powers. I wonder if I make myself clear? All I mean is that I am truly humble in the presence
of art, whether on a cultural level, a primitive level or a child's
level. Spirit can shine through an idiot as well as through a
saint, what! I never turned my back on art; I may have been
defiant, nothing more. I may only have believed (naively) that
art is capable of more than men have dared hope for. In the
same way that I might say God is capable of far worse crimes
than any we mortals can imagine. Praising Him all the while.
But never pretending to *know* Him. 'Let me sing thy praises,
O Lord!' In that spirit.

But the poison I spoke of. . . . The poison was that anybody
or anything could unseat me from my happiness, my deep,
natural inner happiness. I did not want to be a wobbly, as
other men. To sway from joy to despair. The day I came upon
that passage in Nijinsky where he says: 'I want every one to be
like me', I nearly jumped out of my skin. They could have been
my own words. Must one be a complete solipsist or a madman
to speak thus? Often I have asked myself the question.

Naturally it wasn't identity that Nijinsky wanted; he didn't
want to see ten billion Nijinskys all about him. No. He wanted
them to be filled with his divine, radiant, out-going spirit. Is
that not it? Was there any harm in that?

All my rebelliousness, all this crazy tempering with the world,
the divine set-up, or rather the man-made set up, for it was the
human never the cosmic woes which disturbed me, sprang from
my failure to comprehend what people meant—and by people
I mean parents, sweethearts, friends, counselors—when they
urged me to do this or that, become this or that. Let me be,
was all I wanted. Be what I am, no matter how I am. Why is
it that at this moment, and I have thought it a thousand times
to myself, I always summon as proof of the foregoing this image
—of myself as a little boy going down into the street to play,
having no fixed purpose, no particular direction, no especial
friend to seek out, but just divinely content to be going down

into the street to meet what ever might come. In the most bitter arguments, with women, something like this thought always crept in. As though I was yelling my head off to put this simple thought into their heads—'I find life so simple, so good, so easy . . . why must you complicate it?' Or if they said, as they often did—'But how do I know you love me?'—I would become tongue-tied. Such a preposterous accusation to make against me. As if I did not love them! Only, I also loved others too. . . . Not in the way they meant, but in a natural wholesome easy way. Like one loves garlic, honey, wild strawberries. One must not love in this wide, indiscriminate way. One must not have friends who also happen to be traitors, thieves or what not. One must not enjoy a bad movie as much as a good movie. And so on. Clear?

Serenity is when you get above all this, when it doesn't matter what they think, say or want, but when you do as you are, and see God and Devil as one. Then you stop writing, of course. You don't need to play at God or Devil any longer. You've seen through, and the world is always at the level of your vision, of the stuff of your vision. It's when you discover that light is not a manifestation of some physical law but one of the infinite aspects of spirit itself. And there is no light on earth which matches the inner light.

I was going to speak about Homer and the gods, Homer and carnage, Homer and his last minute introductions, Homer the exoskeletonized psychologist . . . but some other time. I am nearly finished with the Iliad. But not with Homer. One thing I am tempted to say in parting . . . at this writing there isn't one character, one god, in the Iliad whom I truly like or admire. Certainly not the two magnificent ones—Hector and Achilles. I know no author who has filled his characters with so many faults—unlovable, unforgivable faults. Enough!

Make what you can of all this! And don't wobble, what!

Cheers!

Henry.

WORKS BY HENRY MILLER*

BOOKS

Tropic of Cancer (Obelisk Press, Paris, 1934).
Aller Retour New York (Obelisk Press, Paris, 1935).
Black Spring (Obelisk Press, Paris, 1936).
Max and the White Phagocytes (Obelisk Press, Paris, 1938).
Tropic of Capricorn (Obelisk Press, Paris, 1939).
Hamlet (with Michael Fraenkel) 2 vols. (Carrefour, Paris–New York, 1939 & 1941).
The Cosmological Eye (New Directions, New York, 1939).
The World of Sex (privately printed, U.S.A., 1940)
The Colossus of Maroussi (The Colt Press, San Francisco, 1941).
The Wisdom of the Heart (New Directions, New York, 1941).
Sunday After the War (New Directions, New York, 1944).
The Air-conditioned Nightmare (New Directions, New York, 1945).
Maurizius Forever (The Colt Press, San Francisco, 1946).
Remember to Remember (New Directions, New York, 1947).
The Smile at the Foot of the Ladder (Duell, Sloan & Pearce, New York, 1948).
Sexus, 2 vols. (Obelisk Press, Paris, 1949).
The Books in My Life (New Directions, New York, 1952).
Plexus, 2 vols. (The Olympia Press, Paris, 1953).
Big Sur and the Oranges of Hieronymus Bosch (privately printed, U.S.A., 1955).
Nights of Love and Laughter, Pocket Book (New American Library of World Literature, New York, 1955).
Days of Love and Hunger, Pocket Book (New American Library of World Literature, New York, 1955).
Rimbaud or the Time of the Assassins (New Directions, New York, 1956).
† *Quiet Days in Clichy* (Olympia Press, Paris, 1956).
A Devil in Paradise, Pocket Book (New American Library of World Literature, New York, 1956).
† *The World of Sex:* text completely rewritten (Olympia Press, Paris, 1957).
The Red Notebook: facsimile edition (Jargon Books, Highlands North Carolina, 1958).
Reunion in Barcelona (Scorpion Press, Northwood, England, 1959).
The Intimate Henry Miller: Pocket Book (New American Library of World Literature, New York, 1959).
The Henry Miller Reader (New Directions, New York, 1959).
† *Nexus:* Vol. I. (Olympia Press, Paris, 1959).

* This list comprises English-language editions only, with names of publishers and dates of first publication in chronological order.

† Not available in English-speaking countries or Communist-controlled countries.

BROCHURES AND PAMPHLETS

What Are You Going To Do About Alf? (Paris, 1935).
Scenario (Obelisk Press, Paris, 1937).
Money and How It Gets That Way (Paris, 1938).
Obscenity and the Law of Reflection (Alicat Book Shop, Yonkers, New York, 1944).
The Plight of the Creative Artist in the U.S.A. (Bern Porter, Berkeley, Calif., 1944).
Murder the Murderer (Bern Porter, Berkeley, Calif., 1944).
The Amazing and Invariable Beauford Delaney (Alicat Bookshop, Yonkers, New York, 1945).
Patchen, Man of Anger and Light (Padell, New York, 1946).
Of, By, and About Henry Miller (Alicat Book Shop, Yonkers, New York, 1947).
The Waters Reglitterized (John Kidis, San Jose, Calif., 1950).
Obscenity and Pornography: Handbook for Censors (Fridtjof-Karla Publications, Michigan City, Indiana, 1958).

MISCELLANEOUS SPECIAL ITEMS

The Angel is my Watermark (Holve-Barrows, Fullerton, Calif., 1944).
Semblance of a Devoted Past (Bern Porter, Berkeley, Calif., 1945).
Henry Miller Miscellanea (Bern Porter, Berkeley, Calif., 1945).
Why Abstract? (with Hilaire Hiler and William Saroyan: New Directions, New York, 1945).
Rimbaud, originally entitled *When Do Angels Cease to Resemble Themselves?* (Part I: New Directions Year Book No. 9, 1946; Part II: New Directions Year Book No 11, 1949). 1946 and 1949 respectively.
Into the Night Life (with Bezalel Schatz: Berkeley, Calif., 1947).

BOOKS AND BROCHURES ABOUT HENRY MILLER

Henry Miller, by Nicholas Moore (Opus Press, Wigginton, England, 1943).
The Happy Rock, a book about Henry Miller by over 25 contributors, including Lawrence Durrell and Alfred Perlès (Bern Porter, Berkeley, Calif., 1946).
Henry Miller, a Chronology and Bibliography, composed and arranged by Bern Porter (Bern Porter, Berkeley, Calif., 1945).
My Friend Henry Miller, by Alfred Perlès (Neville Spearman, London, 1956).
Reunion in Big Sur, by Alfred Perlès (Scorpion Press, Northwood, England, 1959).